EXECUTIVE SUMMARY

Lebanon is a parliamentary republic based on the 1943 National Pact, which apportions governmental authority among a Maronite Christian president, a Shia speaker of the Chamber of Deputies (parliament), and a Sunni prime minister. On October 31, Michel Aoun was elected by parliament to the presidency, ending more than two years of political deadlock. Observers considered the 2009 parliamentary elections peaceful, free, and fair. The parliament postponed subsequent parliamentary elections, granting themselves two extensions, first in 2013 and then again in November 2014. These elections were rescheduled for May 2017.

Civilian authorities maintained control over the armed forces and other security forces, although Palestinian security and militia forces, the designated terrorist group Hizballah, and other extremist elements operated outside the direction or control of government officials.

Following the influx of refugees since the start of the crisis in Syria in 2011, the country experienced increased spillover violence, including several rounds of fighting initiated by the extremist groups Da'esh and al-Nusra Front (Nusra).

The most significant human rights abuses during the year were torture and abuse by security forces, harsh prison and detention center conditions, and limitations on freedom of movement for Palestinian and Syrian refugees.

Other human rights abuses included lengthy pretrial detention; a judiciary subject to political pressure and long delays in trials; violation of citizens' privacy rights; some restrictions on freedoms of speech and press, including intimidation of journalists; some restrictions on freedom of assembly; harassment of Syrian political activists and other refugees; restrictions on citizens' ability to choose their government; official corruption and lack of transparency; widespread violence against women; societal, legal, and economic discrimination against women; societal and legal discrimination against lesbian, gay, bisexual, transgender, and intersex (LGBTI) individuals; trafficking in persons; discrimination against persons with disabilities; systematic discrimination against Palestinian and other refugees and minority groups; killings related to societal violence; restricted labor rights for and abuse of migrant domestic workers; and child labor.

Although the legal structure provides for prosecution and punishment, government officials enjoyed a measure of impunity for human rights abuses.

Despite the presence of Lebanese and UN security forces, Hizballah retained significant influence over parts of the country, and the government made no tangible progress toward disbanding and disarming armed militia groups, including Hizballah. Palestinian refugee camps continued to act as self-governed entities and maintained security and militia forces not under the direction of government officials. Da'esh and Nusra maintained a significant military presence along the country's eastern border, particularly near the city of Arsal, and conducted suicide bombing attacks.

Section 1. Respect for the Integrity of the Person, Including Freedom from:

a. Arbitrary Deprivation of Life and Other Unlawful or Politically Motivated Killings

There were no reports that the government or its agents committed arbitrary or unlawful killings during the year. Islamist extremist groups, however, committed numerous unlawful killings.

The country was increasingly affected by the Syrian crisis, which further polarized its politics, paralyzed many state institutions, generated a massive humanitarian refugee crisis, depressed the economy, inflamed sectarian tensions, and degraded national security. The continued spillover of violence led to the unlawful deprivation of life throughout the country, particularly in Tripoli, Arsal, and the southern suburbs of Beirut, by nonstate actors, including gangs and terrorist organizations.

On June 27, eight suicide bombers attacked the predominantly Christian village of Qaa near the Syrian border, killing five and wounding at least 28 others. There was no official claim of responsibility.

In 2014 clashes erupted between army personnel and Islamist militants aligned with Da'esh and Nusra in Arsal. Nineteen Lebanese Armed Forces (LAF) members and 40 to 45 Syrians and Lebanese died; 90 to 100 individuals were injured. Islamist militants took 29 LAF and Internal Security Forces (ISF) members hostage, executed four, released six, and kept the remainder prisoner. In December 2015 Nusra released 16 Lebanese service members in a prisoner exchange with the LAF; nine service members continued to be held captive by Da'esh.

In 2013 the Special Tribunal for Lebanon (STL), which operated based upon an agreement between the United Nations and the government, indicted Hassan Habib Merhi, a Hizballah member, as a fifth suspect in the 2005 killing of former prime minister Rafik Hariri and 22 other individuals. In 2011 the STL indicted four individuals, Mustafa Amine Badreddine, Hussein Hassan Oneissi, Salim Jamil Ayyash, and Assad Hassan Sabra, all of whom were Hizballah operatives suspected of collaborating in the 2005 killings. Due to the incidents' similar nature and gravity, the STL also established jurisdiction over the 2005 killing of former communist party leader George Hawi and attacks on former ministers Elias Murr and Marwan Hamadeh. Government authorities, however, notified the STL that they were unable to detain or serve the accused with the indictments in that case. In 2014 the STL opened its first trial in the case of Ayyash and other defendants. During the year the government discreetly paid its dues to the STL, despite rumors that the government would forego paying to avoid provoking Hizballah.

b. Disappearance

There were no confirmed reports of politically motivated disappearances by the government during the year.

In December 2015 security forces freed Hannibal Qadhafi, the son of late Libyan leader Muammar Qadhafi, in Baalbek, but it was unclear where or when he had been kidnapped. Media reported that his captors kidnapped him to obtain information about the fate of Imam Moussa Sadr, a prominent Shia cleric, who was last seen in Libya in 1978. At year's end Qaddafi's whereabouts were unknown.

Syrians who fled to Lebanon from civil war, including political activists and other refugees, risked being targeted, harassed, and arrested by Lebanese security services, as well as by others. Syrian opposition activists asserted that Syrian agents in Lebanon targeted them. They claimed they had to operate clandestinely for their protection. Additionally, retaliatory sectarian kidnappings occurred because of Da'esh's and Nusra's actions in Arsal.

c. Torture and Other Cruel, Inhuman, or Degrading Treatment or Punishment

The law does not specifically prohibit all forms of torture or cruel, inhuman, or degrading treatment or punishment, and there were reports security officials employed such practices. The penal code prohibits using acts of violence to obtain a confession or information about a crime, but the judiciary rarely investigated or prosecuted allegations of such acts. According to domestic and international human rights groups, security forces abused detainees and used torture to obtain confessions or encourage suspects to implicate other individuals.

Human rights organizations reported that torture occurred in certain police stations and in the Ministry of Defense's detention facilities. The government denied the use of torture, although authorities acknowledged violent abuse sometimes occurred during preliminary investigations at police stations or military installations where suspects were interrogated without an attorney. Such abuse reportedly occurred in multiple units despite national laws prohibiting judges from accepting confessions extracted under duress.

Reports that the ISF threatened, mistreated, and tortured drug users, persons involved in prostitution, and LGBTI persons in their custody were common. The most common forms of abuse reported were blows from fists, boots, or implements, such as sticks, canes, and rulers. The ISF responded to similar claims in prior years and stated the reports defamed the organization and called for verification of unproven allegations, although evidence in some cases, including video evidence, proved the use of torture in some facilities.

Former prisoners, detainees, and reputable local human rights groups reported that methods of torture and abuse included continuous blindfolding, hanging detainees by wrists tied behind their backs, violent beatings, blows to the soles of the feet, electric shocks, sexual abuse, psychological abuse, immersion in cold water, extended periods of sleep deprivation, being forced to stand for extended periods, threats of violence against relatives, and deprivation of clothing, food, and toilet facilities. Allegations that the ISF specifically targeted the LGBTI community for abuse were common.

Prison and Detention Center Conditions

Prison and detention center conditions were harsh, and prisoners often lacked access to basic sanitation. In some prisons, such as the central prison in Roumieh, conditions were life threatening. Facilities were not adequately equipped for persons with disabilities.

<u>Physical Conditions</u>: As of August there were approximately 6,500 prisoners and detainees, including pretrial detainees and remanded prisoners, in facilities built to hold 3,500 inmates. Roumieh Prison, with a designed capacity of 1,500, held approximately 3,150 persons. Authorities often held pretrial detainees together with convicted prisoners. Authorities held men and women separately in similar conditions, and ISF statistics indicated that 158 minors and 296 women were incarcerated.

Sanitary conditions in overcrowded prisons were poor, and they worsened in Roumieh following a destructive riot in 2011. According to a government official, most prisons lacked adequate sanitation, ventilation, and lighting, and temperatures were not regulated consistently. Prisoners lacked consistent access to potable water (as do many Lebanese citizens). Roumieh prisoners often slept 10 in a room originally built to accommodate two prisoners. Basic medical care at Roumieh improved with better equipment and training, but staffing continued to be inadequate, and working conditions were poor. Additionally, the medical facilities were extremely overcrowded. According to ISF statistics, 13 prisoners died from natural causes during the year. Some nongovernmental organizations (NGOs) complained of authorities' negligence and failure to provide appropriate medical care to prisoners, which may have contributed to some of the deaths. The ISF reported that none died of police abuse and that there were no cases of rape in prisons during the year. On August 22, authorities fined a woman 11,000 Lebanese pounds ($7.33) for alleged slander against the army. She had claimed army officers raped her while in detention in 2013. Authorities detained the woman for a month in 2015 for the alleged slander against the army.

There were reports of female prisoners exchanging sex in return for "favors," such as cigarettes, food, more comfortable conditions in their cells, or a more lenient police report.

<u>Administration</u>: Recordkeeping was not adequate. In many prisons authorities did not release inmates who completed their sentences due to poor recordkeeping. Some juveniles benefitted from alternative sentencing. Although there is a legal means to impose a sentence of probation or supervised release for adults in lieu of incarceration, authorities did not apply it. A person sentenced to imprisonment for more than six months may obtain a sentence reduction upon demonstrating that he had good behavior, that he does not pose a threat to himself or others, and that he met certain conditions depending on the category of crime and the release order. The Commission on the Reduction of Sentences considered sentence reduction

requests. A chamber of the Court of Appeals, which made the final decision on whether to reduce a sentence, reviewed the commission's recommendations.

There were no prison ombudsmen. Authorities did not implement a 2005 law establishing an ombudsman to serve on behalf of citizens. The ISF, however, posted signs in detention facilities stating detainees' rights and had an inspection unit. The minister of interior assigned a general-rank official as the commander of the inspection unit and a colonel-rank official as the commander of the medical and human rights unit. The units were instructed to investigate every complaint. After completing an investigation, authorities transferred the case to the inspector general for action in the case of a disciplinary act or to a military investigative judge for additional investigation. If investigators found physical abuse, the military investigator assigned a medical team to confirm the abuse and the judge ruled at the conclusion of the review. There were no statistics available at year's end regarding the number of complaints, investigations, and disciplinary or judicial actions taken.

Families of prisoners normally contacted the Ministry of Interior to report complaints, although prison directors could also initiate investigations. According to a government official, prison directors often protected officers under investigation.

The ISF's Committee to Monitor Against the Use of Torture and Other Inhuman Practices in Prisons and Detention Centers conducted a minimum of one or two prison visits per week. The parliamentary human rights committee was responsible for monitoring the Ministry of Defense detention center.

Independent Monitoring: The government permitted independent monitoring of prison and detention conditions by local and international human rights groups and the International Committee of the Red Cross (ICRC), and such monitoring took place. The ICRC regularly visited 23 prisons and detention centers.

Nongovernmental entities, such as Hizballah and Palestinian militias, also operated unofficial detention facilities, but no information about these facilities was available.

Improvements: The ISF reported improvements in Roumieh prison that included rehabilitating the jails in the juvenile's building as well as rehabilitating the sewage system, installing new water tanks with a filtering system, completing the rehabilitation of the third floor of Block "D," beginning rehabilitation of the second floor, rehabilitating the main entrance of the prison and installing new equipment, and beginning work on the new private security building. Authorities rehabilitated Zghorta, Halba, and Baalbak prisons and began rehabilitation of Douma prison. Authorities installed power generators in a number of prisons and renovated the entrance of the Qobbeh prison.

d. Arbitrary Arrest or Detention

The law requires judicial warrants before arrests except in cases of active pursuit. Nonetheless, the government arbitrarily arrested and detained persons.

Role of the Police and Security Apparatus

The ISF, under the Ministry of Interior, is responsible for law enforcement. The General Directorate for State Security, reporting to the prime minister, and the Directorate of General Security (DGS), under the Ministry of Interior, are responsible for border control. The LAF, under the Ministry of Defense, is responsible for external security but also may arrest and detain suspects on national security grounds. All of these organizations collected information on groups deemed possible threats to state security. Each security apparatus has its own internal mechanisms to investigate cases of abuse and misconduct. A 2012 ISF code of conduct defines the obligations of ISF members and the legal and ethical standards by which they must abide in performing their duties. Various security forces underwent training on the code. Civilian authorities maintained effective control over security forces. Government security force officials, however, reportedly enjoyed a measure of implicit impunity due to the lack of publicly available information on the outcome of prosecutions. The government lacked mechanisms to investigate and punish abuse and corruption. There are internal complaint mechanisms within the security forces.

In accordance with UN Security Resolutions 425 and 426, the UN Interim Force in Lebanon (UNIFIL) was established in 1978 to confirm the Israeli withdrawal from the southern region of the country, restore peace and security, and assist the government in restoring its authority over its territory. UN Security Resolution 1701 stated UNIFIL was to monitor (per UN resolutions) cessation of hostilities between Israel and Hizballah after their 2006 war, accompany the LAF in deploying in the south, assist in providing humanitarian access to civilians and safe return of displaced, and assist the government in securing its borders.

Arrest Procedures and Treatment of Detainees

The law generally requires a warrant for arrest and provides the right to a medical examination and referral to a prosecutor within 48 hours of arrest. If authorities hold a detainee longer than 48 hours without formal charges, the arrest is considered arbitrary, and authorities must release the detainee or request a formal extension. The code of criminal procedures provides that a person may be held in police custody for investigation for 48 hours, unless the investigation requires additional time, in which case the period of custody may be renewed for another 48 hours.

By law bail is available in all cases regardless of the charges, although the amounts required may be prohibitively high.

The code of criminal procedures also states that from the moment of arrest a suspect or the subject of a complaint has the right to contact a member of his family, his employer, an advocate of his choosing, an acquaintance, or an interpreter, and undergo a medical examination on the approval of the general prosecutor. It does not mention, however, whether a lawyer may attend preliminary questioning with the judicial police. In practical terms the lawyer may not attend the preliminary questioning with judicial police. Under the framework of the law, it is possible for a suspect to be held at a police station for hours before being granted the right to contact an attorney. If the suspect lacks the resources to obtain legal counsel, authorities must provide free legal aid. The law does not, however, require the judicial police to inform an individual who lacks legal counsel that one may be assigned through the Bar Association, whether in Beirut or Tripoli.

The law does not require authorities to inform individuals they have the right to remain silent. Many provisions of the law simply state that if the individual being questioned refuses to make a statement or remains silent, this should be recorded and that the detainee may not be "coerced to speak or to undergo questioning, on pain of nullity of their statements."

The law states the period of detention for a misdemeanor may not exceed two months. This period may be extended by a maximum of two additional months. The initial period of custody may not exceed six months for a felony, but the detention may be renewed. Excluded from this protection are suspects accused of homicide or with a previous criminal conviction, drug crimes, endangerment of state security, violent crimes, and crimes involving terrorism.

Officials responsible for prolonged arrest may be prosecuted on charges of depriving personal freedom, but authorities rarely filed charges. The law requires authorities to inform detainees of the charges filed against them. A suspect caught in the act of committing a crime must be referred to an examining judge, who decides whether to issue an indictment or order the release of the suspect.

Authorities failed to observe many provisions of the law, and government security forces, as well as extralegal armed groups such as Hizballah, continued the practice of extrajudicial arrest and detention, including incommunicado detention. Additionally, the law permits military intelligence personnel to make arrests without warrants in cases involving military personnel or involving civilians suspected of espionage, treason, or weapons possession.

Arbitrary Arrest: According to local NGOs, cases of arbitrary detention continued; however, most victims chose not to report violations against them. NGOs reported that most cases involved vulnerable groups such as refugees, migrant workers, drug users, and LGBTI individuals. Civil society groups reported authorities frequently detained foreign nationals arbitrarily.

Pretrial Detention: As of December 2015, ISF reported 3,853 of the 6,502 persons in prison were in pretrial detention. The Office of the UN High Commissioner for Human Rights expressed concern about arbitrary pretrial detention without access to legal representation and refused to support construction of prisons until authorities resolved the serious problem of arbitrary pretrial detention. According to a study by the Lebanese Center for Human Rights, detainees spent one year on average in pretrial detention prior to sentencing. Individuals accused of murder spent on average 3.5 years in pretrial detention. Many Salafist prisoners remained in prolonged pretrial detention, including detainees from the Nahr el-Bared fighting in 2007.

State security forces and autonomous Palestinian security factions subjected Palestinian refugees to arbitrary arrest and detention.

Detainee's Ability to Challenge Lawfulness of Detention before a Court: Lawyers infrequently challenged the lawfulness of their client's detention, despite a defendant's rights to do so. As a result the defense mainly focused on presenting evidence and arguments to challenge the prosecutor's verdict.

e. Denial of Fair Public Trial

Although the constitution provides for an independent judiciary, authorities subjected the judiciary to political pressure, particularly in the appointment of key prosecutors and investigating magistrates. Influential politicians and intelligence officers intervened at times and used their influence and connections to protect supporters from prosecution. Persons involved in routine civil and criminal proceedings sometimes solicited the assistance of prominent individuals to influence the outcome of their cases.

Trial Procedures

Defendants are presumed innocent until proven guilty. Trials are generally public, but judges have the discretion to order a closed court session. Defendants have the right to be present at trial, to consult with an attorney in a timely manner, and to question witnesses against them. Defendants may present witnesses and evidence, and their attorneys have access to government-held evidence relevant to their cases. Defendants have the right not to be compelled to testify or confess guilt; they have the right of appeal. Defendants have the right to free interpretation; however, interpreters were rarely available.

The Military Court has jurisdiction over cases involving the military as well as those involving civilians accused of espionage, treason, weapons possession, and draft evasion. Civilians may be tried on security charges, and military personnel may be tried on civil charges. The Military Court has a permanent tribunal and a cassation tribunal. The latter hears appeals from the former. A civilian judge chairs the higher court. Defendants on trial under the military tribunal have the same procedural rights as defendants in ordinary courts. Human rights groups expressed concerns about the trial of civilians in military courts, the extent to which they were afforded full due process, and the lack of review of verdicts by ordinary courts.

Because of an agreement struck between the Lebanese government and late Palestinian leader Yasser Arafat, Lebanese security forces do not enter Palestinian camps; they remain outside the entrance and check vehicles and identification. As a result the camps, particularly Ain el-Helweh, had the reputation of being lawless enclaves, and authorities stated that foreign and local jihadists found refuge within them.

The Palestinian factions that theoretically provided security in the camps often fought each other for control, and these groups generally controlled the justice systems in the camps. Governance varied greatly, with some camps under the control of joint Palestinian security forces, while local militia strongmen heavily influenced others. Palestinian groups in refugee camps operated an autonomous and arbitrary system of justice outside the control of the state. For example, local popular committees in the camps attempted to resolve disputes through informal mediation methods but occasionally transferred those accused of more serious offenses (for example, murder and terrorism) to state authorities for trial. Several Palestinian factions formed a joint security force to help maintain stability and security within the Ain el-Helweh camp, but Islamist groups increasingly challenged this force for control of the camp in 2015. Beginning in August a large number (reportedly more than 30) of extremist militants surrendered to the LAF outside Ain el-Helweh because of reported cooperation between the army and Palestinian factions within the camp.

Political Prisoners and Detainees

There were no reports of political prisoners or detainees.

Civil Judicial Procedures and Remedies

There is an independent judiciary in civil matters, but plaintiffs seldom submitted civil lawsuits seeking damages for government human rights violations to it. During the year there were no examples of a civil court awarding a person compensation for such violations. There is no regional mechanism to appeal adverse domestic human rights decisions. The country has reservations on individual complaints under any human rights treaty, body, or special procedures. Appeals to international human rights bodies are accessible only after exhausting all domestic remedies.

f. Arbitrary or Unlawful Interference with Privacy, Family, Home, or Correspondence

The law prohibits such actions, but authorities frequently interfered with the privacy of persons regarded as enemies of the government. There were reports security services monitored private e-mail and other digital correspondence.

The law provides for the interception of telephone calls with prior authorization from the prime minister at the request of the minister of interior or minister of defense.

Militias and non-Lebanese forces operating outside the area of central government authority also frequently violated citizens' privacy rights. Various nonstate actors, such as Hizballah, used informer networks and telephone monitoring to obtain information regarding their perceived adversaries.

LAF forces raiding Syrian refugee settlements caused destruction of physical property while making arrests and in some cases forced refugees to move their informal settlements away from LAF positions.

Personal status was legally handled by religious courts, which applied religious laws of the various confessions and occasionally interfered in family matters such as child custody in the case of divorce. Refugee birth registrations require families to register birth certificates with Lebanese ministries, which remained inaccessible because the ministries require proof of legal residence and legal marriage.

g. Abuses in Internal Conflict

After suicide bombings in the village of al-Qaa on June 27, media reported that some security personnel used excessive force to detain refugees during raids looking for the bombing suspects; however, other sources, including the Office of the UN High Commissioner for Refugees (UNHCR), claimed the media reports were exaggerated and not widespread.

Section 2. Respect for Civil Liberties, Including:

a. Freedom of Speech and Press

The law provides for freedom of speech and press and stipulates that restrictions may be imposed only under exceptional circumstances. The government generally respected these rights, but there were some restrictions, particularly regarding political and social issues.

<u>Freedom of Speech and Expression</u>: Individuals were free to criticize the government but legally prohibited from publicly criticizing the president (a post that was vacant throughout the year) and foreign leaders. Authorities also hindered the expression of certain views.

On May 30, authorities arrested Nabil al-Halabi, a lawyer and human rights activist, over his Facebook posts criticizing government officials. In his Facebook posts, Halabi accused Interior Ministry officials of corruption and possible complicity with persons arrested by ISF agents on March 27 in connection with sex trafficking of Syrian women.

<u>Press and Media Freedoms</u>: Independent media outlets were active and expressed a wide variety of views. The majority of outlets had political affiliations, which hampered their ability to operate freely in areas dominated by other political groups and affected their reporting. Local, sectarian, and foreign interest groups financed media outlets that reflected their views. The law restricts the freedom to issue, publish, and sell newspapers. Publishers must apply for and receive a license from the Ministry of Information in consultation with the press union.

The law governing audiovisual media bans live broadcasts of unauthorized political gatherings and certain religious events and prohibits the broadcast of "any matter of commentary seeking to affect directly or indirectly the well-being of the nation's economy and finances, material that is propagandistic and promotional, or promotes a relationship with Israel." Media outlets must receive a license from the Council of Ministers, based on a recommendation by the minister of information, to broadcast direct and indirect political news and programs. The law also prohibits broadcasting programs that seek to affect the general system, harm the state or its relations with Arab and other foreign countries, or have an effect on the well-being of such states. The law also prohibits the broadcast of programs that seek to harm public morals, ignite sectarian strife, or insult religious beliefs.

On March 8, the appeals panel of the STL reversed the contempt conviction of Karma Khayat, the deputy head of news of the television news station al-Jadeed, and upheld the acquittal of the station, in connection with the broadcast of information concerning the identity of confidential witnesses. The court also overturned a 10,000 euro ($11,000) fine Khayat was sentenced to pay.

On July 15, the STL found *al-Akhbar* newspaper and its editor in chief, Ibrahim al-Amin, guilty of contempt of court. Authorities had charged al-Amin and *al-Akhbar*'s parent company with contempt of court and obstruction of justice after the newspaper published photographs and personal details of 32 confidential witnesses set to appear before the tribunal investigating the 2005 assassination of former Prime Minister Rafik Hariri.

<u>Violence and Harassment</u>: On April 1, protesters attacked and vandalized the Beirut offices of pan-Arab *Ash-Sharq al-Awsat* newspaper, citing their objection to a cartoon published by the newspaper that they claimed insulted the country. The offending cartoon depicted the Lebanese flag with the caption "The Lebanese

State… April Fool's." The attackers also accused the journalists working in *Ash-Sharq al-Awsat* of being non-Lebanese. Leading to the attack, there was a significant social media campaign against the newspaper. Authorities apprehended all but one of the attackers but released them a few days later on bail. The court case was pending at year's end.

On June 17 and 18, Ali al-Amine, the publisher of the Janoubia online portal, received threats via social media platforms by Hizballah supporters.

<u>Censorship or Content Restrictions</u>: The law permits, and authorities selectively used, prior censorship of pornographic material, political opinion, and religious material considered a threat to national security or offensive to the dignity of the head of state or foreign leaders. The DGS reviewed and censored all foreign newspapers, magazines, and books to determine admissibility into the country. Political violence and extralegal intimidation led to self-censorship among journalists.

The law includes guidelines regarding materials deemed unsuitable for publication in a book, newspaper, or magazine. Any violation of the guidelines could result in the author's imprisonment or a fine.

Authors could publish books without prior permission from the DGS, but if the book contained material that violated the law, the DGS could legally confiscate the book and put the author on trial. In some cases authorities might deem the offending material a threat to national security. Authorities did not take such offenses to trial based on the publication law, but rather on the basis of criminal law or other statutes. Publishing a book without prior approval that contained unauthorized material could put the author at risk of a prison sentence, fine, and confiscation of the published materials.

Authorities from any of the recognized religious groups could request the DGS to ban a book. The government could prosecute offending journalists and publications in the publications court.

The government's strained political relations with certain Arab countries where major satellite television operators were based curtailed several Lebanese satellite channels' ability to broadcast their content. For example, on April 6, Egyptian satellite provider Nilesat stopped broadcasting al-Manar to its subscribers, claiming the channel violated its contract by transmitting programs promoting sectarian division. During the same month, Nilesat announced it was withdrawing from the country and cancelling its uplinking satellite services due to issues related to the contract with the government. Their move affected the satellite broadcasts of all local Lebanese channels, obliging them to find other alternatives. Negotiations between the government and Nilesat over Nilesat's services continued at year's end.

On April 1, the Saudi-owned, Dubai-based al-Arabiya news channel announced that it had "restructured" its operations in the country and closed its offices in Beirut "due to the difficult circumstances and challenges on ground, and due to al-Arabiya's concern for the safety of its own employees and those employed by its providers." Al-Arabiya provided no further justification for the closure.

In November 2015 Saudi-based satellite communications operator Arabsat stopped broadcasting Beirut-based al-Mayadeen satellite channel and stopped broadcasting Beirut-based al-Manar satellite channel in December 2015. Media reported that authorities blocked these channels for their criticism of Saudi Arabia's policies.

Libel/Slander Laws: The 1991 security agreement between the Lebanese and Syrian governments, still in effect at year's end, contained a provision prohibiting the publication of any information deemed harmful to the security of either state.

On January 16, the criminal court decided to terminate the case of journalist Dima Sadek due to insufficient evidence. In November 2015 authorities summoned Sadek to appear before the criminal court, rather than the court of publications, on allegations of defamation and slander against Hizballah during a televised interview with Hizballah members.

Nongovernmental Impact: Radical Islamist groups sometimes sought to inhibit freedom of the press through coercion and threat of violence.

Internet Freedom

The law does not restrict access to the internet. There was a perception among knowledgeable sources, however, that the government monitored e-mail, Facebook, Twitter, blogs, and internet chat rooms where individuals and groups engaged in the expression of views. The government reportedly censored some websites to block online gambling, pornography, religiously provocative material, extremist forums, and Israeli websites, but there were no verified reports the government systematically attempted to collect personally identifiable information via the internet.

In the absence of laws governing online media and activities on the internet, the ISF's Cyber Crimes Unit and other state agencies summoned journalists, bloggers, and activists to question them about tweets, Facebook posts, and blog posts critical of political figures.

Restrictions on freedom of speech concerning government officials applied to social media communications on Facebook and Twitter, which authorities considered a form of publication rather than private correspondence. There were also reports of political groups intimidating individuals and activists for their online posts. On February 2, the Cyber Crimes Unit summoned journalist Mohamad Alloush concerning his report about a case of corruption in public administration. On February 8, authorities raided the Saida residence of photographer Ali Khalifeh and later summoned him for interrogation for "distorting the image of former Prime Minister Rafik Hariri and disseminating it via social media."

Internet access was available and widely used by the public. According to the Internet World Statistics, internet penetration was 75.9 percent in 2016.

Academic Freedom and Cultural Events

There are no government restrictions specific to academic freedom, but libel and slander laws apply.

The majority of private universities enjoyed freedom of expression, and students were free to hold student elections and organize cultural, social, and political activities. The Lebanese University, which is the country's only public institution of higher learning, does not have such freedoms, particularly on the campuses that host students affiliated with the Shia Hizballah and Amal Movement.

Observers considered the university's main campus in the area of Hadath as a stronghold for youth affiliated with the two influential Shia parties in the country. There were many incidents where students affiliated with these two parties silenced their political opponents, particularly civil society activists.

In February students from a civil society movement withdrew from student elections following pressure and harassment from Amal Movement. It was reported that Amal Movement students pressured the director of the School of Business and Economics to provide them the telephone numbers of the students in the civil society movement to ruin their electoral campaign. The director was attacked by Amal Movement students on February 15 because he rejected their request to provide personally identifiable information without authorization of the university's president. Authorities suspended the student elections following this incident.

On June 16, Mohamad Fahes, a student affiliated with Hizballah, in the Lebanese University's School of Sciences, posted statements on his Facebook page calling upon his fellow female students to refrain from wearing short skirts on campuses located in Hizballah areas, including the main campus and southern branches; he threatened to force what he called "the nude student" to put on more clothes. Although no physical action was reported, Fahes' calls spurred anger among bloggers and social media activists. Many students denounced his calls, underscoring the students' freedom of opinion and behavior.

The government censored films, plays, and other cultural events. The DGS reviewed all films and plays and prohibited those deemed offensive to religious or social sensibilities. The DGS's decision-making process lacked transparency and was influenced by the opinions of religious institutions and political groups. Cultural figures and those involved in the arts practiced self-censorship to avoid being detained or refused freedom of movement. On July 15, NGO Legal Agenda publicized that the DGS banned three films--*Carol* by Todd Haynes, *I Say Dust* by Darine Hoteit, and *My Name Is* by Karl Haddad--because the films dealt with LBGTI issues and declared that these films aimed "to promote homosexuality." The documentary *In This Land Lay Graves of Mine* by Reine Mitri was scheduled to be shown at the American University of Beirut on October 27, but the DGS banned it from both public and private screenings because of alleged sectarian content.

b. Freedom of Peaceful Assembly and Association

Freedom of Assembly

The constitution provides for the freedoms of assembly and association with some conditions established by law, but the government sometimes restricted this right. Organizers are required to obtain a permit from the Interior Ministry three days prior to any demonstration. In previous years the ministry sometimes did not grant permits to groups that opposed government positions, but there were no known examples of this restriction being applied during the year.

Security forces occasionally intervened to disperse demonstrations, usually when clashes broke out between opposing protesters.

On August 16, protesters, including members of the Kataeb party students, blocked the entrance to the Bourj Hammoud landfill to prevent dump trucks from entering the site. Security forces deployed in the area and tried to convince them to open the road. The protesters remained in the road and forced the dump's closure for a month. On September 11, the protesters suspended their actions. Security forces and demonstrators were both peaceful throughout the month-long protest.

In August 2015 police clashed with civil society activists from the "You Stink" movement over similar waste management issues. After the clashes authorities arrested many of the protesters involved in the violence and rioting. Ultimately, authorities opened three case files after the protests. Although the details of two of the cases were unknown and investigations were in progress, in the third case authorities charged 14 persons of suspected riot assembly. Authorities charged three of the 14 with attacking the ISF, and another three of the 14 were charged with destroying public property. As of November the case was still open, although none of the accused were in detention. The hearing for the case file was set for January 2017.

NGOs that advocated for women's rights, particularly those focused on combating domestic violence with organized protests and media campaigns, were met with some interference by security forces.

Freedom of Association

The constitution provides for freedom of association with some conditions established by law, and the government generally respected the law.

No prior authorization is required to form an association, but the Interior Ministry must be notified for it to be recognized as legal, and the ministry must verify that the organization respects public order, public morals, and state security. The ministry sometimes imposed additional inconsistent restrictions and requirements and withheld approval. In some cases the ministry sent notification of formation papers to the security forces to initiate inquiries on an organization's founding members. Organizations must invite ministry representatives to any general assembly where members vote on bylaws, amendments, or positions on the board of directors. The ministry must then validate the vote or election. Failure to do so may result in the dissolution of the organization by a decree issued by the Council of Ministers.

The cabinet must license all political parties (see section 3).

Independent NGOs in areas under Hizballah's sway faced harassment and intimidation, including social, political, and financial pressures. Hizballah reportedly paid youth who worked in "unacceptable" NGOs to leave the groups.

c. Freedom of Religion

See the Department of State's *International Religious Freedom Report* at www.state.gov/religiousfreedomreport/.

d. Freedom of Movement, Internally Displaced Persons, Protection of Refugees, and Stateless Persons

The law provides for freedom of internal movement, foreign travel, emigration, and repatriation, and the government generally respected these rights for citizens but placed extensive limitations on the rights of Palestinian refugees and Syrian, Iraqi, and other refugee populations. As of September 1, UNHCR registered 1,033,513 Syrian refugees and, as of June 30, registered 21,873 refugees or asylum seekers from countries other than Syria, most of whom were from Iraq. The UN Relief and Works Agency for Palestine Refugees in the Near East (UNRWA) provided assistance to Palestinian refugees registered in Lebanon (while approximately 458,000 individuals registered refugees with UNRWA Lebanon, the estimated number of Palestinian refugees actually living in Lebanon was between 260,000 and 280,000. UNRWA also provided services to Palestinian refugees from Syria (PRS) who fled to Lebanon because of the conflict in Syria and registered with UNRWA in Lebanon. PRS in Lebanon numbered 30,675, according to an UNRWA count completed in July.

Abuse of Migrants, Refugees, and Stateless Persons: Multiple NGOs and UNHCR shared reports of sexual harassment and exploitation of refugees by government employers and landlords, including paying workers below the minimum wage, working excessive hours, debt bondage, and pressuring families into early marriage for their daughters or nonconsensual sex.

The government lacked the capacity to provide adequate protection for refugees. Refugees regularly reported abuse by members of political parties and gangs, often without official action in response. Additionally, LAF raids on settlements often resulted in harassment and destruction of personal property.

According to UNHCR, domestic courts often sentenced Iraqi and African refugees registered with UNHCR to one month's imprisonment and fines instead of deporting them for illegal entry. After serving their sentences, most refugees remained in detention unless they found employment sponsors and the DGS agreed to release them in coordination with UNHCR.

In-country Movement: The government maintained security checkpoints, primarily in military and other restricted areas. Hizballah also maintained checkpoints in certain Shia-majority areas. Government forces were usually unable to enforce the law in the predominantly Hizballah-controlled southern suburbs of Beirut and did not typically enter Palestinian refugee camps. According to UNRWA, Palestinian refugees registered with the Interior Ministry's Directorate of Political and Refugee Affairs could travel from one area of the country to another. The directorate, however, had to approve the transfer of registration of residence for refugees who resided in camps. UNRWA stated the directorate generally approved such transfers.

Syrian refugees registered with UNHCR must pay a renewal fee of 300,000 Lebanese pounds ($200) for each person age 15 or above each 12 months if the person wishes to remain in the country lawfully as a refugee. Syrian refugees who arrived in the country after January 2015 must have entered with a Lebanese sponsor. In light of decreasing refugee resources, renewal fees were prohibitively expensive, and most refugees had difficulty affording the fees. In addition to the fee, refugees had to provide legal housing documents and a notarized pledge not to work in the first half of the year. In May authorities replaced the housing document by a registration certificate issued by UNHCR. In July authorities also replaced the pledge not to work with a pledge to abide by the country's laws. With respect to the latter, this instruction was slowly and unevenly being implemented throughout the country. Due to the residency fee and, in some cases, failure to obtain a Lebanese sponsor, many refugees were unable to renew their legal documents, which significantly affected their freedom of movement owing to regular arrests at checkpoints. While authorities released most detainees within a few days, a few reported their treatment in detention and reasons for release. Some of the refugees met by embassy officers said authorities required them to pay fines before being released. By March 31, the United Nations' joint household assessment of more than 100,000 refugee families indicated that 85 percent of refugee households had at least one member without legal status. A number of refugees reported that the UNCHR registration certificate was not sufficient to renew their residency, as authorities asked them to produce a Lebanese sponsor, which in turn led to heightened risks of exploitation and abuse. Syrian refugees who entered the country irregularly or lacked Syrian passports or national identity documents reportedly cannot obtain residency permits with either a sponsor or UNHCR registration.

Similarly, despite DGS announcements that PRS could renew their legal immigration status for three months upon payment of 300,000 Lebanese pounds ($200) per year, implementation was inconsistent and the cost prohibitively high for most PRS. At the end of October 2015, the DGS began issuing several circulars allowing free-of-charge three-month extensions of residency documents for PRS who entered the country legally, but many PRS reportedly did not approach the DGS due to fear of arrest and deportation. While "departure orders" for those without legal residency status in the country were not actively enforced, authorities issued departure orders, and detention of PRS without legal status remained a risk.

In September the DGS issued a new circular stating that residency was free for PRS who had been in the country for less than one year, and the 300,000 Lebanese pound ($200) per person fee for persons 15 years and older that must be renewed every six months was waived for the first year. Upon further discussion with the DGS, authorities informed UNRWA that free-of-charge residency visas would be available for a year following the date of the last renewal of their residency, while those who had not renewed their residency during the last year would have to pay the 300,000 Lebanese pound ($200) fees. Based on UNRWA's field monitoring and legal assistance services, UNRWA observed inconsistency and discrepancy between this information and the policies DGS offices implemented across the country. Authorities asked the majority of PRS approaching DGS offices to pay the 300,000 Lebanese pound ($200) fees despite having renewed their residency visa within the past year.

Internally Displaced Persons

Fighting in 2007 destroyed the Nahr el-Bared Palestinian refugee camp, displacing 30,000 Palestinian refugees. As of July 31, UNRWA reported that 8,854 Palestinian refugees (2,193 families) returned to newly constructed apartments in Nahr el-Bared camp, while another 12,416 remained displaced. Many of the displaced resided in areas adjacent to the camp or in other areas of the country where UNRWA services were available. Officials anticipated that a further 2,224 residents could return to the rebuilt camp by April 2017.

Protection of Refugees

<u>Access to Asylum</u>: The law does not provide for the granting of asylum or refugee status, and the country is not a party to either the 1951 convention relating to the status of refugees or the 1967 protocol.

According to a study conducted by the American University of Beirut in 2015, 65 percent of Palestinian refugees in the country lived in poverty, compared to 90 percent of PRS. The study estimated unemployment at 23 and 52 percent for Palestinian refugees and PRS, respectively. Palestinian refugees were prohibited from accessing public health and education services or owning land and were barred from employment in many fields, making refugees dependent upon UNRWA as the sole provider of education, health care, and social services. A 2010 labor law revision expanded employment rights and removed some restrictions on Palestinian refugees; however, this law was not fully implemented, and Palestinians remained barred from working in most skilled professions, including almost all those that require membership in a professional association.

As of June 30, there were 1,033,513 Syrians refugees registered with UNHCR. This total did not include Syrian refugees who arrived in the country in 2015, as UNHCR Lebanon suspended new registration of Syrian refugees after January 2015 in accord with the government's instructions. There were no formal refugee camps in the country for Syrians. Many Syrian refugees resided with host families, in unfinished buildings, or in temporary tent settlements. More than two-thirds of Syrian refugees lived in extreme poverty. A UN assessment of more than 4,000 refugee households found that an estimated 70 percent lived below the Lebanese extreme poverty line of 5,790 Lebanese pounds ($3.86) per day. According to the study, the refugees borrowed to cover even their most basic needs, including rent, food, and health care, putting nearly 90 percent of them in debt.

In January 2015 new government regulations banned the entry of all Syrian refugees unless they qualified for undefined "humanitarian exceptions." During the year the government accepted Syrians seeking asylum only if they qualified under the "humanitarian exceptions" that the Ministry of Social Affairs reviewed on a case-by-case basis. These exceptions included unaccompanied and separated children, persons with disabilities, medical cases, and resettlement cases under extreme humanitarian criteria.

In 2014 authorities began restricting entry into the country for PRS. For PRS to enter from Syria, they must be in possession of an officially validated plane ticket and visa for travel to a third country or have a confirmed embassy appointment in Lebanon. Authorities generally granted PRS who have all the required documentation a 24-hour transit visa. UNRWA reported that the DGS issued some PRS departure orders despite their having paid the renewal fee. Legal status in Lebanon was critical for protection, as it ensured refugees could pass through checkpoints, including to and from camps, complete civil registration processes, and access and remain within the educational system.

There was also a limited influx of Iraqi refugees who entered the country seeking to escape violence from the fight against Da'esh. As of August there were 18,542 Iraqi refugees registered with UNHCR. As of June 30, UNHCR also registered 3,530 refugees or asylum seekers from Sudan and other countries.

Freedom of Movement: Authorities imposed curfews in a number of municipalities across the country, allegedly to improve security of all communities. Some international observers raised concerns that these measures may be discriminatory and excessive since authorities almost always enforced them on Syrian refugees only.

Employment: During the year authorities began requiring Syrian refugees who wished to obtain residency permits to pledge to abide by the country's laws, under which Syrians may work only in agriculture, construction, and cleaning.

A 2010 amendment to the social security law created a special account to provide end-of-service indemnities or severance pay to Palestinian refugees who retired or resigned. These benefits were available only to Palestinians working in the legal labor market. Palestinians did not benefit from national sickness and maternity funds or the family allowances fund. UNRWA continued to bear the cost of any medical, maternity, or family health-care expenses (excluding worker's compensation). The law provides for benefits only from 2010 onward. According to an American University of Beirut study, less than 3.3 percent of Palestinian refugees in country had an official employment contract by a public notary, which enables them to apply for a work permit.

Access to Basic Services: The government did not consider local integration of any refugees a viable solution. After Syrians and Palestinians, Iraqis were the third-largest group of refugees in the country.

The law considers UNRWA-registered Palestinian refugees to be foreigners, and in several instances they experienced worse treatment than other foreign nationals. UNRWA has the sole mandate to provide health, education, social services, and emergency assistance to the 458,000 registered Palestinian refugees residing in the country. The amount of land allocated to the 12 official Palestinian refugee camps in the country has changed only marginally since 1948, despite a four-fold increase in the population. Consequently, most Palestinian refugees lived in overpopulated camps, some of which were heavily damaged during past conflicts. In accordance with agreements with the government, Palestine Liberation Organization (PLO) security committees provided security for refugees in the camps, with the exception of the Nahr el-Bared camp.

A comprehensive, multi-year plan to rebuild the Nahr el-Bared camp and surrounding communities in eight stages began in 2008 and was in process, but remaining reconstruction was not fully funded, and a shortfall of 2,066,097 Lebanese Pounds ($137 million) remained at year's end. Of the 27,000 Palestinians originally displaced following the crisis, authorities expected approximately 22,000 to return.

A 2001 amendment to a 1969 decree barring persons explicitly excluded from resettling in the country from owning land and property was designed to exclude Palestinians from purchasing or inheriting property. Palestinians who owned and registered property prior to the 2001 law entering into force are able to bequeath it to their heirs, but individuals who were in the process of purchasing property in installments were unable to register the property.

Palestinian refugees residing in the country could not obtain citizenship and were not citizens of any other country. Palestinian refugee women married to Lebanese citizens were able to obtain citizenship after one year of marriage. According to Lebanese nationality law, the father transmits citizenship to children. Palestinian refugees, including children, had limited social and civil rights and no access to public health, education, or other social services. Children of Palestinian refugees faced discrimination in birth registration, and many had to leave school at an early age to earn an income.

Palestinians who fled Syria to Lebanon since 2011 received limited basic support from UNRWA, including food aid, cash assistance, and winter assistance. Authorities permitted their children to enroll in UNRWA schools and access UNRWA health clinics. UNRWA's verification exercise in late summer found that there were approximately 30,000 PRS recorded with the agency, which reflected a decrease of more than 10,000 PRS in the country over the previous 12 months.

The Ministry of Education and Higher Education facilitated the enrollment of more than 157,000 Syrian students in public schools in the 2015-16 academic year, and enrollment continued at year's end. Donor funding was available to support 200,000 children to enroll; however, the UN Children's Fund (UNICEF) estimated there were approximately 379,000 school-age Syrian refugee children (ages five to 17). Donor funding to UN agencies covered school-related expenses, such as school fees, books, and uniforms. Syrian refugees had access to many government and private health centers and local clinics for primary care services, and UN agencies and NGOs funded the majority of associated costs. Syrian refugees had access to a limited number of UNHCR-contracted hospitals for emergency care.

Iraqi refugees had access to both the public and private education systems. UNHCR reported that more than 600 Iraqi children registered in public schools, and it provided grants to the children's families to help defray the costs associated with attending school. Iraqi refugees also had access to the primary health-care system. UNHCR, through NGOs, provided secondary health care.

Temporary Protection: The country is not a signatory to the Refugee Convention and does not recognize refugees in Lebanon. Authorities termed Syrians "displaced." While the government consistently reaffirmed its commitment to the principle of nonrefoulement with respect to Syrians, this commitment does not apply to refugees and asylum seekers from other countries, who remained at concrete risk of forced repatriation, particularly those without resettlement prospects.

According to UNHCR, authorities detained 226 refugees and non-Syrian asylum seekers through August, of whom 148 remained in detention at the end of the year. Through August the DGS deported eight persons despite UNHCR's interventions.

UNHCR continued to intervene with authorities to request the release of persons of concern who were detained either beyond their sentence or for illegal entry or presence.

Stateless Persons

Citizenship is derived exclusively from the father, resulting in statelessness for children of a citizen mother and a noncitizen father when registration under the father's nationality is not possible. This discrimination in the nationality law particularly affected Palestinians and increasingly Syrians from female-headed households. Additionally, some children born to Lebanese fathers may not have had their births registered due to a lack of understanding of the regulations or administrative obstacles. The problem was compounded since nonnational status was a hereditary circumstance that stateless persons pass to their children. There were no official statistics on the size of the stateless population.

Approximately three thousand Palestinian refugees were not registered with UNRWA or the government. Also known as undocumented Palestinians, most of these individuals moved to the country after the expulsion of the PLO from Jordan in 1971. Palestinians faced restrictions on movement and lacked access to fundamental rights under the law. Undocumented Palestinians, who were not registered in other fields, were not necessarily eligible for the full range of services provided by UNRWA. Nonetheless, in most cases UNRWA provided primary health care, education, and vocational training services to undocumented Palestinians. The majority of undocumented Palestinians were men, many of them married to UNRWA-registered refugees or Lebanese citizen women, who could not transmit refugee status or citizenship to their husbands or children.

The Directorate of Political and Refugee Affairs continued to extend late registration to Palestinian refugee children under age 10. It previously was the directorate's policy to deny late birth registration to Palestinian refugee children who were above age two. Children between age 10 and 20 were registered only after the following were completed a DNA test, an investigation by the DGS, and the approval of the directorate.

Approximately 1,000 to 1,500 of an estimated 100,000 Kurds living in the country lacked citizenship, despite decades of family presence in the country. Most were descendants of migrants and refugees who left Turkey and Syria during World War I but were denied citizenship to preserve the country's sectarian balance. The government issued a naturalization decree in 1994, but high costs and other obstacles prevented many individuals from acquiring official status. Some individuals who received official status had their citizenship revoked in 2011, because of a presidential decree. Others held an "ID under consideration" document without date or place of birth.

Stateless persons lacked official identity documents that would permit them to travel abroad and could face difficulties traveling internally, including detention for not carrying identity documents. They had limited access to the regular employment market and no access to many professions. Additionally, they could not access public schools or public health-care facilities, register marriages or births, and own or inherit property.

Section 3. Freedom to Participate in the Political Process

Although the law provides citizens the ability to choose their government in free and fair periodic elections conducted by secret ballot and based on universal and equal suffrage, lack of government control over parts of the country, defects in the electoral process, prolonged extension of parliament's mandate, and corruption in public office significantly restricted this ability. The president and parliament nominate the prime minister, who, with the president, chooses the cabinet.

Elections and Political Participation

Recent Elections: Observers concluded that the 2009 parliamentary elections were generally free and fair, with minor irregularities, such as instances of vote buying. The NGO Lebanese Transparency Association reported its monitors witnessed election fraud through cash donations on election day in many electoral districts. In 2013 parliament postponed legislative elections to November 2014 and later rescheduled them for June 2017.

Municipal elections were held on May 8, 15, 22, and 29, and constituted the first nationwide elections since the 2010 municipal elections. Although the elections were largely free and fair, observers present at some polling centers witnessed irregularities including party agents present inside polling stations, no official preprinted ballots, instances of campaigning by party agents around and inside the polling center and polling stations, and electoral bribery.

Political Parties and Political Participation: All major political parties and numerous smaller ones were almost exclusively based on confessional affiliation, and parliamentary seats were allotted on a sectarian basis.

Participation of Women and Minorities: No laws limit the participation of women and members of minorities in the political process; however, there were significant cultural barriers to women's participation in politics. Prior to 2004 no woman held a cabinet position, and there were only four female ministers since then. During the year one woman served in the cabinet. Only four of 128 members of parliament were women, and all were close relatives of previous male members. With a few notable exceptions, leadership of political parties effectively excluded women, limiting their opportunities for high office.

Minorities participated in politics to some extent. Regardless of the number of its adherents, every government-recognized religion, except Coptic Christianity, Ismaili Islam, and Judaism, was allocated at least one seat in parliament. Three parliamentarians representing minorities (one Syriac Orthodox Christian and two Alawites) were elected in the 2009 elections. None of the minority parliamentarians were women. These groups also held high positions in government and the LAF. Since refugees are not citizens, they have no political rights. An estimated 17 Palestinian factions operated in the country, generally organized around prominent individuals. Most Palestinians lived in refugee camps that one or more factions controlled. Palestinian refugee leaders were not elected, but there were popular committees that met regularly with UNRWA and visitors.

Section 4. Corruption and Lack of Transparency in Government

Although the law provides criminal penalties for official corruption, the government did not implement the law effectively, and officials often engaged in corrupt practices with impunity and on a wide scale. Government security officials, agencies, and police were subjected to laws against bribery and extortion. The lack of strong enforcement limited the law's effectiveness.

Corruption: Observers widely considered government control of corruption to be poor. Types of corruption generally encountered included systemic patronage; judicial failures, especially in investigations of politically motivated killings; electoral fraud facilitated by the absence of preprinted ballots; and bribery. Bribes customarily accompanied bureaucratic transactions. In addition to regular fees, customers paid bribes for driver's licenses, car registrations, or residential building permits. Syrian refugees reportedly paid bribes to shopkeepers or municipal officials for a variety of services, for example, to receive consignment of aid or facilitate their registration.

Financial Disclosure: The law requires the president of the republic, the president of the Chamber of Deputies, the president of the Council of Ministers, as well as ministers, members of parliament, and judges to disclose their financial assets in a sealed envelope deposited at the Constitutional Council, but the information is not made available to the public. They must also do the same when they leave office.

Heads of municipalities disclose their financial assets in a sealed envelope at the Ministry of Interior, and civil servants deposit their sealed envelopes at the Civil Servants Council, but the information is also not available to the public. If a case is brought to the State Council for noncompliance, the State Council will take judiciary administrative sanctions consisting of terminating the tenure of the incumbent.

Since parliament had not passed a budget since 2005, there was limited parliamentary or auditing authority oversight of revenue collection and expenditures.

Public Access to Information: There are no laws regarding public access to government documents, and the government generally did not respond to requests for documents.

Section 5. Governmental Attitude Regarding International and Nongovernmental Investigation of Alleged Violations of Human Rights

A number of domestic and international human rights groups generally operated without government restriction, investigating and publishing their findings on human rights cases. Government officials generally were not responsive to these groups' views, and there was limited or no accountability for human rights violations.

Government Human Rights Bodies: The parliamentary Committee on Human Rights struggled to advance legislative proposals to make legal changes to guide ministries in protecting specific human rights or, for example, improving prison conditions. The Ministry of Interior has a human rights department to enhance and raise awareness about human right issues within the ISF, train police officers on human right standards, and monitor and improve prison conditions. The ministry staffed the department with two officers, two sergeants, and an information technology specialist, in addition to the department's head. The department was not adequately resourced. Its leadership maintained high standards of professionalism, but due to the integrated structure, the department's independence could not be assured.

In 2014 the ISF launched a revised complaint mechanism allowing citizens to track complaints and receive notification of investigation results. Citizens may file formal complaints against any ISF officer in person at a police station, through a lawyer, by mail, or online through the ISF website. At the time a complaint is filed, the filer receives a tracking number that may be used to check the status of the complaint throughout the investigation. The complaint mechanism provides the ISF the ability to notify those filing complaints of the results of its investigation.

The LAF has a human rights unit that engaged in human rights training through the Department of Defense's Defense Institute of International Legal Studies and other organizations. The unit worked to ensure the LAF operated in accordance with major international human rights conventions and coordinated human rights training in LAF training academies. The LAF human rights unit also worked with international NGOs to coordinate human rights training and policies and requested the creation of legal advisor positions to embed with LAF combat units and advise commanders on human rights and international law during operations. The unit also has responsibility for coordinating the LAF's efforts to combat antitrafficking in persons. The LAF also recently responded to requests for information on alleged human rights allegations by opening new investigations and provided updated information on those investigations.

Section 6. Discrimination, Societal Abuses, and Trafficking in Persons

Women

Rape and Domestic Violence: The law criminalizes rape. While the government effectively enforced the law, its interpretation by religious courts precluded full implementation of civil law in all provinces. Rape and domestic violence were underreported. The minimum prison sentence for a person convicted of rape is five years, or seven years for raping a minor. According to the penal code, the state would not prosecute a rapist and would nullify his conviction if the rapist married his victim. The law does not criminalize spousal rape. According to the domestic NGO Enough Violence and Exploitation (KAFA), 80 percent of domestic-violence victims the NGO assisted suffered spousal rape.

During the year husbands killed a number of women in domestic violence cases. On August 22, Prosecutor General Samir Hammoud appealed a five-year sentence handed down to Mohammad Nhaily for beating his wife, Manal Assi, to death in 2014. On July 14, the criminal court gave Nhaily a mitigated sentence based on the penal code, which allows for reduced punishment if a crime occurred as a result of extreme outrage caused by "dangerous and wrongful action committed by the victim." Hammoud rejected this argument, saying that the criminal court misinterpreted and wrongly implemented the language of the penal code.

The law criminalizes domestic violence, but it does not specifically provide protection for women. The law does not criminalize spousal rape but rather the use of threats or violence to claim a "marital right to intercourse," and it does not criminalize the nonconsensual violation of physical integrity. The maximum sentence under this law is 25 years' imprisonment if one of the spouses commits homicide.

A 2010 UN Population Fund (UNFPA) assessment estimated there were high rates of domestic violence in the country. Despite a law that sets a maximum sentence of 10 years in prison for battery, some religious courts may legally require a battered wife to return to her home despite physical abuse. Foreign domestic workers, usually women, often were mistreated, abused, and in some cases raped or placed in slavery-like conditions. Some police, especially in rural areas, treated domestic violence as a social, rather than criminal, matter.

The government provided legal assistance to domestic violence victims who could not afford it, and police response to complaints submitted by battered or abused women improved. The NGOs Lebanese Council to Resist Violence against Women and KAFA offered counseling and legal aid and raised awareness about the problem. During the year KAFA assisted victims in 538 cases of violence, the majority of which concerned domestic violence.

Sexual Harassment: The law prohibits sexual harassment, but authorities did not enforce the law effectively, and it remained a widespread problem. According to the UNFPA, the labor law does not explicitly prohibit sexual harassment in the workplace; it merely gives a male or female employee the right to resign without prior notice from his or her position in the event that an indecent offense is committed towards the employee or a family member by the employer or his or her representative, without any legal consequences for the perpetrator. The penal code and the criminal procedure cite legal consequences.

Reproductive Rights: Couples and individuals have the right to decide the number, spacing, and timing of their children; manage their reproductive health; and have the information and means to do so, free from discrimination, coercion, or violence.

Some women in rural areas faced social pressure on their reproductive choices due to long-held conservative values. According to 2015 estimates from the UNFPA, while 63 percent of women between the ages of 15 and 49 used contraceptives, only 40 percent used a modern method. While there was no reliable data on the contraceptive prevalence rate for Syrian refugees, the UNFPA supported a study to assess the unmet need in family planning and estimated the rate as well as family planning requirements among the Syrians in the country for the next three to four years. A study carried out in 2013-14 by the UNFPA and partners among a sample of 1,000 Syrian displaced youth estimated that while 45 percent of youth knew about contraceptive methods, 39 percent of those surveyed thought that contraceptives should not be used. Of those who have had children since arriving in the country, 41 percent did not intend to have more children but were not using any form of contraception.

Discrimination: Women suffered discrimination under the law and in practice. Social pressure against women pursuing some careers was strong in some parts of society. Men sometimes exercised considerable control over female relatives, restricting their activities outside the home or their contact with friends and relatives. In matters of child custody, inheritance, and divorce, personal status laws provide unequal treatment across the various confessional court systems but generally discriminate against women. For example, Sunni civil courts applied an inheritance law that provides a son twice the inheritance of a daughter. Religious law on child custody matters favors the father in most instances. Nationality law also discriminates against women, who may not confer citizenship to their spouses and children, although widows may confer citizenship to their minor children. By law women may own property, but they often ceded control of it to male relatives due to cultural reasons and family pressure.

The law provides for equal pay for equal work for men and women, but in the private sector there was discrimination regarding the provision of benefits. Only 26 percent of women, compared with 76 percent of men, were in the formal labor force, and these women earned on average 61 percent of what men earned for comparable work.

The Women's Affairs Division in the Ministry of Social Affairs undertook some projects to address sexual or gender-based violence, such as providing counseling and shelter for victims and training ISF personnel to combat violence in prisons.

The National Commission for Lebanese Women is the highest governmental body addressing women's issues.

Children

<u>Birth Registration</u>: Citizenship is derived exclusively from the father, which may result in statelessness for children of a citizen mother and noncitizen father who may not transmit his own citizenship (see section 2.d.). If a child's birth is not registered within the first year, the process for legitimizing the birth is long and costly, often deterring families from registration. Syrian refugees faced numerous challenges registering their births because of the country's complicated registration system. Authorities did not permit refugees without valid residency papers to register their child's birth, preventing them from obtaining necessary documents for passports.

Some refugee children and the children of foreign domestic workers also faced obstacles to equal treatment under the law. NGOs reported discrimination against them, although some could attend public school.

<u>Education</u>: Education for citizens is free and compulsory through the primary phase. Noncitizen children, including those born of noncitizen fathers and citizen mothers and refugees, lack this right. Certain public schools had quotas for noncitizen children, but there were no special provisions for children of female citizens, and spaces remained subject to availability. Boys and girls had nearly equal rates of primary education, with women outnumbering men in secondary and tertiary education. Authorities permitted Syrian refugee children to enroll in public schools; the Ministry of Education and Higher Education facilitated the enrollment of more than 157,000 Syrian students in public schools in the 2015-16 academic year, and enrollment continued at year's end. UNICEF and the Ministry of Education and Higher Education accelerated learning program continued during the year, enrolling more than 11,000 students in remedial classes to be grade-level ready for formal enrollment as of May. The ministry did not recognize informal education, limiting the number of opportunities for refugee children to receive accredited education or a pathway to enroll once they achieved grade-level proficiency.

<u>Child Abuse</u>: According to a 2012 study by KAFA in partnership with the Ministry of Social Affairs, more than 885,000 children were victims of psychological abuse, of whom 738,000 were also victims of physical abuse and 219,000 were victims of sexual abuse. The Ministry of Social Affairs had a hotline to report cases of child abuse.

Syrian refugee children were vulnerable to child labor and exploitation.

Children reportedly joined local gangs engaged in sectarian violence in the northern part of the country.

Early and Forced Marriage: The legal age for marriage is 18 for men and 17 for women. Confessionally determined personal status law governs family matters, and minimum ages acceptable for marriage differ accordingly. UNHCR reported early and forced marriage was common in the Syrian refugee community. According to a study conducted by the Heartland Alliance in 2014, the marriages were not official but usually endorsed by sheikhs in the refugee community, often encouraged with a bribe. These sheikhs were not linked to the country's Sunni family courts, and the marriages had no legal standing.

Sexual Exploitation of Children: The penal code prohibits and punishes commercial sexual exploitation, child pornography, and forced prostitution. Prescribed punishment for commercial sexual exploitation of a person under age 21 is imprisonment for one month to one year and fines between 50,000 and 500,000 Lebanese pounds ($33 and $333). The maximum sentence for commercial sexual exploitation is two years' imprisonment. The minimum age for consensual sex is 18, and statutory rape penalties include hard labor for a minimum of five years and a minimum of seven years' imprisonment if the victim is younger than 15. Imprisonment ranges from two months to two years if the victim is between ages 15 and 18. The government generally enforced the law. As of August 31, the ISF investigated 15 cases of human trafficking involving nine victims of sexual exploitation and referred them to the judiciary. On March 27 and 29, the ISF broke up a sex trafficking ring, which exploited primarily 45 Syrian women and girls in Beirut and arrested 16 perpetrators involved in the ring. In 2015 the DGS investigated 52 suspected cases of trafficking involving nonpayment of wages, physical abuse, and rape or sexual abuse. Additionally, the Ministry of Justice reported investigating 93 suspected traffickers, of which the government charged and prosecuted 71 under the antitrafficking law. Authorities found 33 of these offenders guilty of trafficking and referred them to the courts for trial. The cases involved forced labor, forced child street begging, and sex trafficking.

Displaced Children: The Ministry of Education and Higher Education opened 200,000 places in the public school system to Syrian refugee children in the 2015-16 academic year. As of November 2015, 157,000 Syrian refugee children had enrolled in public schools. NGOs often used informal education to assist students not performing at grade-level, but the ministry opposed nonformal education, which limited access to education for refugees and prompted many NGOs to terminate programs.

Some refugee children lived and worked on the street. Given the poor economic environment, limited freedom of movement, and little opportunity for livelihoods for adults, many Syrian refugee families relied on children to be able to earn money for the family. Refugee children were at greater risk of exploitation and child labor, since they had greater freedom of movement compared to their parents, who often lacked residency permits.

International Child Abductions: The country is not a party to the 1980 Hague Convention on the Civil Aspects of International Child Abduction. See the Department of State's *Annual Report on International Parental Child Abduction* at travel.state.gov/content/childabduction/en/legal/compliance.html.

Anti-Semitism

At year's end there were approximately 100 Jews living in the country and six thousand registered Jewish voters who lived abroad but had the right to vote in parliamentary elections.

The Jewish Community Council reported that acts of vandalism against the cemetery in Beirut continued during the year. Vandals also threw construction rubble and trash into the cemetery. The council reported the abuse to the security forces, but authorities took no action. Rooms, shops, and a gas station were built on the land of the Jewish cemetery in Tripoli, and a lawsuit was filed; however, authorities took no action by year's end.

The national school curriculum materials did not contain materials on the Holocaust.

Trafficking in Persons

See the Department of State's *Trafficking in Persons Report* at www.state.gov/j/tip/rls/tiprpt/.

Persons with Disabilities

Although prohibited by law, discrimination against persons with disabilities continued. Employment law defines a "disability" as a physical, sight, hearing, or mental disability. The law stipulates that persons with disabilities fill at least 3 percent of all government and private-sector positions, provided such persons fulfill the qualifications for the position; however, no evidence indicated the government enforced the law. Employers are legally exempt from penalties if they provide evidence no otherwise qualified person with disabilities applied for employment within three months of advertisement. The law mandates access to buildings by persons with disabilities, but the government failed to amend building codes. Many persons with mental disabilities received care in private institutions, several of which the government subsidized.

The Ministry of Social Affairs and the National Council of Disabled is responsible for protecting the rights of persons with disabilities. According to the president of the Arab Organization of Disabled People, little progress had occurred since parliament passed the law on disabilities in 2000. Approximately 100 relatively active but poorly funded private organizations provided most of the assistance received by persons with disabilities.

Depending on the type and nature of the disability, children with a disability may attend mainstream school. Due to a lack of awareness or knowledge, school staff often did not identify a specific disability in children and could not adequately advise parents. In such cases children often repeated classes or dropped out of school.

The Ministry of Education and Higher Education stipulates for new school building construction: "Schools should include all necessary facilities in order to receive the physically challenged." Nonetheless, the public school system was ill-equipped to accommodate students with disabilities. Problems included a poor regulatory framework; poor infrastructure that was not accessible to persons with disabilities; curricula that did not include material to assist children with disabilities; laboratories and workshops that lacked the equipment required for children with disabilities; laboratories that lacked space and access for persons with disabilities, especially those using wheelchairs; teaching media and tools that relied increasingly on computers and audiovisual material that were not accessible to students with disabilities, including students who were blind, deaf, and those with physical disabilities; and a lack of accessible transportation to and from schools.

Some NGOs (often managed by religious entities) offered education and health services for children with disabilities. The Ministry of Social Affairs contributed to the cost, although the ministry often delayed payments to the organizations. According to the ministry, it supported school attendance, vocational training, and rehabilitation for approximately eight thousand persons in 2014.

In the May municipal elections, access for persons with disabilities and older persons was a significant issue. Most polling centers had multiple floors with no elevators. ISF officers helped, and at times carried, some voters with disabilities into the polling stations. Some voting booths were on elevated levels, and some voters required assistance to reach the elevated polling booths.

National/Racial/Ethnic Minorities

Lebanese of African descent attributed discrimination to the color of their skin and claimed harassment by police, who periodically demanded to see their papers. Foreign Arab, African, and Asian students, professionals, and tourists reported being denied access to bars, clubs, restaurants, and private beaches.

Syrian workers, usually employed as manual laborers and construction workers, continued to suffer discrimination, as they did following the 2005 withdrawal of Syrian forces from the country. Many municipalities enforced a curfew on Syrians' movements in their neighborhoods in an effort to curb an increased number of robberies and to control security.

Acts of Violence, Discrimination, and Other Abuses Based on Sexual Orientation and Gender Identity

Official and societal discrimination against LGBTI persons persisted. There is no all-encompassing antidiscrimination law to protect LGBTI persons. The law prohibits "unnatural sexual intercourse," an offense punishable by up to one year in prison but rarely applied; however, it often resulted in a fine. The Ministry of Justice did not keep records on these infractions. Enforcement of the law varied and often occurred through occasional police arrests. There were, however, no reports authorities imprisoned anyone for violation of this law during the year.

Various NGOs, including Helem, Arab Foundation for Freedoms and Equality (AFE), LebMash, and Marsa, hosted regular meetings in a safe house, provided counseling services, and carried out advocacy projects for the LGBTI community.

The government did not collect information on official or private discrimination in employment, occupation, housing, statelessness, or lack of access to education or health care based on sexual orientation or gender identity, and individuals who faced problems were reluctant to report incidents due to fear of additional discrimination. There were no government efforts to address potential discrimination.

NGOs claimed LGBTI persons underreported incidents of violence and abuse due to negative social stereotypes. Observers received reports from LGBTI refugees of physical abuse by local gangs, which the victims did not report to the ISF. Observers referred victims to UNHCR-sponsored protective services. There was one confirmed case of a man who was physically abused and threatened with death by throwing him from the third floor of a building in Beirut because of his LGBTI status. It was unclear if the perpetrator was a family member or an acquaintance.

A local NGO report on Lebanese attitudes towards LGBTI found clear instances of negative stereotypes, rejection, and, although to a lesser extent, readiness for violence.

Most reports of abuse came from transgender women. This circumstance was highlighted by graphic accounts of transwomen's testimonies in the "Transpowerment" project implemented by AFE and Marsa. The project highlighted that transgender women faced employment discrimination due to the inconsistency between official documentation and gender self-presentation, which rendered personnel paperwork practically impossible due to constraints related to social security registration, payroll, and opening bank accounts.

In September 2015 the Court of Appeals granted a transgender man the right to rectify his legal status in the civil registry after taking into account his psychological, sexual, moral, and social status.

HIV and AIDS Social Stigma

HIV/AIDS is stigmatized due to sensitivities about extramarital relations. Few who contracted the disease did so in the course of homosexual relations, which are also taboo. The main challenge facing AIDS patients, in addition to stigma and discrimination, was that many were unable to pay for regular follow-up tests that the Ministry of Public Health does not cover. The law requires the government to offer treatment to all residents who are AIDS patients rather than deporting foreigners who carry the disease.

NGOs such as Marsa, Soins Infirmiers et Developpement Communautaire, and Vivre Positif offered free testing services to HIV patients. According to Marsa, patients that tested positive for HIV risked losing their medical insurance--and in some cases their jobs--because of the stigma surrounding the disease. Patients were often reluctant to test themselves because the test gives rise to fear of infection and social stigma.

Other Societal Violence or Discrimination

As in previous years, there were reports of incidents of societal violence and interreligious strife. Observers reported Shia militias, most notably Hizballah, harassed unfamiliar refugees entering territories under their control. The rise of Da'esh, Nusra, and other extremist groups led to repeated fighting between the LAF and these groups. Political leaders across the country condemned the action of extremist groups.

Section 7. Worker Rights

a. Freedom of Association and the Right to Collective Bargaining

The law provides for the right of private-sector workers to form and join trade unions, bargain collectively, and strike but places a number of restrictions on these rights. The Ministry of Labor must approve the formation of unions, and it controlled the conduct of all trade union elections, including election dates, procedures, and ratification of results. The law permits the administrative dissolution of trade unions and bars trade unions from political activity. Unions have the right to strike after providing advance notice to and receiving approval from the local governor. Organizers of a strike (at least three of whom must be identified by name) must notify the governor of the number of participants in advance and the intended location of the strike, and 5 percent of a union's members must take responsibility for maintaining order during the strike.

There are significant restrictions on the right to strike. The labor law excludes public-sector employees, domestic workers, and agricultural workers; therefore, they neither have the right to strike nor to join and establish unions. The law prohibits public-sector employees from any kind of union activity, including striking, organizing collective petitions, or joining professional organizations. Despite this prohibition, public-sector employees succeeded in forming leagues of public school teachers and civil servants that created the Union of Coordination Committees (UCC), which along with private school teachers, demanded better pay and working conditions.

The law protects the right of workers to bargain collectively, but a minimum of 60 percent of workers must agree on the goals beforehand. Collective bargaining agreements must be ratified by two-thirds of union members at a general assembly. The Union of Syndicates of Bank Employees had requested the Association of Banks to renegotiate the collective agreement for more than a year, although the association had yet to do so. Collective agreements for the Port of Beirut and the American University of Beirut Medical Center employees were still in force, while the port workers union was preparing to negotiate a new agreement.

The law prohibits antiunion discrimination. Under the law, when employers misuse or abuse their right to terminate a union member's contract, including for union activity, the worker is entitled to compensation and legal indemnity and may institute proceedings before a conciliation board. The board adjudicates the case, after which an employer may be compelled to reinstate the worker, although this protection was available only to the elected members of a union's board. Anecdotal evidence showed widespread antiunion discrimination, although this issue did not receive significant media coverage. Most flagrant abuses occurred in banking, private schools, retail businesses, daily and occasional workers, and the civil service. The government and ruling political parties interfered in the elections of the teachers and civil servants leagues, succeeding in removing an active UCC leadership that aimed to transform itself into a genuine trade union structure. The founding members of the domestic workers' union are under scrutiny within the country. The general security agency detained Sunjana Rana and deported her on 10 December. Roja Limbu was arrested December 5 and was still in detention at the end of the year.

By law foreigners with legal resident status may join trade unions. The migrant law permits migrant workers to join existing unions (regardless of nationality and reciprocity agreements) but denies them the right to form their own unions. They do not enjoy full membership as they may neither vote in trade union elections nor run for union office. Certain sectors of migrant workers, such as migrant domestic workers, challenged the binding laws supported by some unions by forming their own autonomous structures that act as unions, although the Ministry of Labor had not approved them.

Palestinian refugees generally may organize their own unions on an individual basis. Because of restrictions on their right to work, few refugees participated actively in trade unions. While some unions required citizenship, others were open to foreign nationals whose home countries had reciprocity agreements with Lebanon.

The government's enforcement of applicable laws was weak, including with regard to prohibitions on antiunion discrimination.

Freedom of association and the right to collective bargaining were not always respected. The government and other political actors interfered with the functioning of worker organizations, particularly the main federation, the General Confederation of Lebanese Workers (CGTL). The CGTL is the only national confederation recognized by the government, although several unions boycotted and unofficially or officially broke from the CGTL and no longer recognized it as an independent and nonpartisan representative of workers. The UCC, a grouping of public and private teachers as well as civil servants, largely overshadowed the CGTL, notably in pushing the government to pass a promised revised salary scale. Although UCC strikes and demonstrations prompted the government to send the revised salary scale proposal to parliament, parliament had yet to approve it. With a new UCC board elected in 2015, its activities decreased considerably.

Antiunion discrimination and other instances of employer interference in union functions occurred. Some employers fired workers in the process of forming a union before the union could be formally established and published in the official gazette. There was no progress on enacting a draft labor code, which had been under discussion since 2008.

There was widespread anecdotal evidence of arbitrary dismissals of Lebanese, being replaced by non-Lebanese, across economic and productive sectors. This was mainly in the form of Syrian refugees allegedly replacing Lebanese in some sectors. There were no official statistics to quantify the scale of these dismissals.

b. Prohibition of Forced or Compulsory Labor

The law prohibits forced or compulsory labor, but the government did not effectively enforce the law, although the government made some efforts to prevent or eliminate it. The law does not criminally prohibit debt bondage.

Children, foreign workers employed as domestic workers, and other foreign workers sometimes worked under forced labor conditions. The law provides protection for domestic workers against forced labor, but domestic work is excluded from protections under the labor law and vulnerable to exploitation. In violation of the law, employment agencies and employers routinely withheld foreign workers' passports, especially in the case of domestic workers, sometimes for years. According to the Beirut Bar Association, authorities jailed one employer for a year for withholding an employee's passport in 2015. To mitigate this practice, the DGS began returning passports to the worker rather than the employer at immigration. According to NGOs assisting migrant workers, some employers withheld salaries for the duration of the contract, which was usually two years.

Also see the Department of State's *Trafficking in Persons Report* at www.state.gov/j/tip/rls/tiprpt/.

c. Prohibition of Child Labor and Minimum Age for Employment

The minimum age for employment is 14, and the law prescribes the occupations that are legal for juveniles, defined as children between ages 14 and 18. The law requires juveniles to undergo a medical exam by a doctor certified by the Ministry of Public Health to assure they are physically fit for the type of work they are asked to perform. The law prohibits employment of juveniles for more than seven hours per day or from working between 7 p.m. and 7 a.m., and it requires one hour of rest for work lasting more than four hours. The law, updated by a decree on the Worst Forms of Child Labor, prohibits specific types of labor for juveniles, including informal "street labor." It also lists types of labor that, by their nature or the circumstances in which they are carried out, are likely to harm the health, safety, or morals of children under 16, as well as types of labor that are allowed for children over 16, provided they are offered full protection and adequate training.

The Ministry of Labor is responsible for enforcing child labor requirements through its Child Labor Unit. Additionally, the law charges the Ministry of Justice, the ISF, and the Higher Council for Childhood (HCC) with enforcing laws related to child trafficking, including commercial sexual exploitation of children and the use of children in illicit activities. The HCC is also responsible for referring children held in protective custody to appropriate NGOs to find safe living arrangements. The Ministry of Labor employed approximately 90 labor inspectors, whom are also called upon to undertake child labor inspections.

Overall, the government did not enforce child labor laws effectively, in part because of inadequate resources. The penal code calls for penalties for those who violate child labor laws ranging from a 250,300 Lebanese pound ($167) fine and one to three months' imprisonment up to closure of the offending establishment. Advocacy groups did not consider these punishments sufficient deterrents.

The government made efforts to prevent child labor and remove children from such labor during the year. Throughout the year the HCC held awareness campaigns in schools and workshops for social workers and journalists who cover child-related issues.

Child labor occurred, including in its worst forms. While up-to-date statistics on child labor were unavailable, anecdotal evidence suggested the number of child workers rose during the year and that more children worked in the informal sector, including commercial sexual exploitation, as UNHCR noted (see section 6, Children).

Child labor, including among refugee children, was predominantly concentrated in the informal sector, including in small family enterprises, mechanical workshops, carpentry, construction, manufacturing, industrial sites, welding, agriculture including in the production of tobacco and fisheries. Anecdotal evidence also suggested child labor was prevalent in Palestinian refugee camps and among Iraqi refugees and Romani communities, and most prevalent in Syrian refugee communities. Some children were involved in the worst forms of child labor, such as street work including begging, selling goods, polishing shoes, and washing car windows, as well as forced labor, sometimes as a result of human trafficking. The International Labor Organization noted abuses involving the use, recruitment, and exploitation of children in political protests and militant activities in the northern region of the country and some areas of Beirut.

Also see the Department of Labor's *Findings on the Worst Forms of Child Labor* at www.dol.gov/ilab/reports/child-labor/findings/.

d. Discrimination with Respect to Employment and Occupation

The law provides for equality among all citizens and prohibits discrimination based on race, gender, disability, language, or social status. The law does not specifically provide for protection against discrimination based on sexual orientation, gender identity, HIV status, or other communicable diseases.

Although the government generally respected these provisions, they were not enforced in some areas, especially in economic matters, and aspects of the law and traditional beliefs discriminated against women. Discrimination in employment and occupation occurred with respect to women, persons with disabilities, foreign domestic workers, and LGBTI and HIV-positive persons (see section 6).

The law provides for equal pay for equal work for men and women, but in the private sector there was discrimination regarding the provision of benefits. Only 26 percent of women, compared with 76 percent of men, were in the formal labor force, and these women earned on average 61 percent of what men earned for comparable work (see section 6, Women).

Although prohibited by law, discrimination against persons with disabilities continued. Employment law defines a "disability" as a physical, sight, hearing, or mental disability. The law stipulates that persons with disabilities fill at least 3 percent of all government and private-sector positions, provided such persons fulfill the qualifications for the position; however, no evidence indicated that the government enforced the law.

Migrant workers and domestic workers faced employment hurdles that amounted to discrimination (see section 7. e.).

e. Acceptable Conditions of Work

The legal minimum wage, last raised in 2012, was 675,000 Lebanese pounds ($450) per month in the public and private sectors.

The law prescribes a standard 48-hour workweek with a weekly rest period that must not be less than 36 consecutive hours. The law stipulates 48 hours work as the maximum per week in most corporations except agricultural enterprises. A 12-hour day is permitted under certain conditions, including a stipulation that overtime pay is 50 percent higher than pay for normal hours. The law does not set limits on compulsory overtime. The law includes specific occupational health and safety regulations and requires employers to take adequate precautions for employee safety.

Domestic workers are not covered under the labor law or other laws related to acceptable conditions of work. Such laws also do not apply to those involved in work within the context of a family, day laborers, temporary workers in the public sector, or workers in the agricultural sector.

The Ministry of Labor is responsible for enforcing regulations related to acceptable conditions of work but did so unevenly. The ministry employed approximately 90 enforcement officials made up of both inspectors and assistant inspectors, as well as administrators and technicians, who handle all inspections of potential labor violations. The number of inspectors, available resources, and legal provisions were not sufficient to deter violations, nor was there political will for proper inspections in other cases. Interference with inspectors affected the quality of inspections and issuance of fines for violators was common. The law stipulates that workers may remove themselves from situations that endanger their health or safety without jeopardy to their employment, although government officials do not protect employees who exercised this right.

Workers in the industrial sector worked an average of 35 hours per week, while workers in other sectors worked an average of 32 hours per week. Some private-sector employers failed to provide employees with family and transportation allowances as stipulated under the law and did not register them with the National Social Security Fund (NSSF).

Some companies did not respect legal provisions governing occupational health and safety in specific sectors, such as the construction industry. Workers could report violations to the CGTL, Ministry of Labor, NSSF, or through their respective unions. In most cases they preferred to remain silent due to fear of dismissal.

Violations of wage, overtime, and occupational health and safety standards were most common in the construction industry and among migrant workers, particularly with foreign domestic workers.

Foreign migrant workers arrived in the country through local recruitment agencies and source-country recruitment agencies. Although the law requires recruitment agencies to have a license from the Ministry of Labor, the government did not adequately monitor their activities. A sponsorship system tied foreign workers' legal residency to a specific employer, making it difficult for foreign workers to change employers. If employment was terminated, a worker lost residency. This circumstance made many foreign migrant workers reluctant to file complaints to avoid losing their legal status.

There was no official minimum wage for domestic workers. Official contracts stipulated a wage ranging from 225,000 to 450,000 Lebanese pounds ($150 to $300) per month for domestic workers, depending on the nationality of the worker. A unified standard contract, which was registered with the DGS for the worker to obtain residency, granted migrant domestic workers some labor protections. The standard contract covered uniform terms and conditions of employment, but the section covering wages was completed individually.

Some employers mistreated, abused, and raped foreign domestic workers, who were mostly of Asian and African origin. Domestic workers often worked long hours and, in many cases, did not receive vacations or holidays. Victims of abuse may file civil suits or seek other legal action, often with the assistance of NGOs, but most victims, counseled by their embassies or consulates, settled for an administrative solution that usually included monetary compensation and repatriation.

Authorities did not prosecute perpetrators of abuses against foreign domestic workers for a number of reasons, including the victims' refusal to press charges and lack of evidence. Authorities settled an unknown number of other cases of nonpayment of wages through negotiation. According to source-country embassies and consulates, many workers did not report violations of their labor contracts until after they returned to their home countries, since they preferred not to stay in the country for a lengthy judicial process.

While licensed businesses and factories strove to meet international standards for working conditions with respect to occupational safety and health, conditions in informal factories and businesses were poorly regulated and often did not meet these standards. The Ministry of Industry is responsible for enforcing regulations to improve safety in the workplace. The regulations require industries to have three types of insurance (fire, third-party, and workers' policies) and to implement proper safety measures. The ministry has the authority to revoke a company's license if its inspectors find a company noncompliant, but there was no evidence this occurred.

The law requires businesses to adhere to safety standards, but the law was poorly enforced and did not explicitly permit workers to remove themselves from dangerous conditions without jeopardy to their continued employment. Workers can ask to change their job or be removed from an unsafe job without being affected, as per the labor code. The government, however weakly implemented the law due to lack of governance, the weak role of the trade union movement, corruption, and lack of trade union rights.